How to do a Kruger Safari

By Philip Law

This book is dedicated to my family.
Firstly, to my wife Hannah who continues to support my passion for Kruger; to my son Thomas and daughter Emily – I look forward to our visits together; to my Mum, Dad and sister who have always enjoyed Kruger with me.
Your love and support has made this book possible.

Table of Contents

Foreword

It has been said many times that visiting Africa touches your soul, and for many the wild places of South Africa provide a connection to your inner-self that brings you back time and time again. Taken on a visit as a young child more than thirty years ago, it is the Kruger National Park that is this anchor for me. You may be planning a once in a lifetime trip or the Kruger may have become a family tradition. This book is designed for both the first time and repeat visitor. It aims to give the reader an idea of how to plan a self-guided safari to Kruger, what to expect on safari and routes that may give you the best chance of seeing the widest variety of animal and bird life. I hope that it will help to instil a love of Kruger in all that read this book and visit the national park. I hope that you will have the opportunity to visit each of the places mentioned in this book and have as much luck and pleasure as I have had. Remember though, that much about game viewing is down to the luck of being in the right place.

Philip Law

How to use this book

This book is organised into sections. In the first section I highlight information that you should know before you plan and go on your trip. This includes all kinds of information about the history of Kruger, how to get there, the kind of car that you need, how to book and the weather that you might expect during your visit. There are also some ideas on how to be safe around the wildlife that you are viewing. In section two you will find maps to help you plan where to stay and which roads to travel on whilst you are there. Each camp is described in section 3 to help you to get a feel for what to expect and there is a handy distance to chart so you know how far apart each of the camps are. Whilst in Kruger you will need some ideas of how to spend your time. These are found in section four, including some suggestions of game viewing routes that will give you a good chance of seeing a wide variety of animal and plant life, including the big five. In the final section you will find more tips relating to wildlife photography. Throughout the book you will find photographs of the animals and places of Kruger. All were taken within the boundaries of this wonderful National Park.

Section one: before you go.

1.1 The park in context.

Location

South Africa's world-renowned wilderness area, the Kruger National Park, is found in the north east of the country, between the Drakensberg Mountains and Mozambique. This lowveld region spans the provinces of Mpumalanga in the south and Limpopo to the north. Comparable in size to the countries of Israel and Wales, the Kruger covers around 2 million hectares. It is approximately 354km long and averages 54km in width.

History

The Kruger National Park was born out of the Sabie and Shingwedzi game reserves that had been proclaimed by the then president of the Transvaal republic, Paul Kruger, at the turn of the 20th century. The two reserves were merged when land in between them was purchased by the state and this area was proclaimed as the Kruger National Park in 1926. A century later, the 1.5 million annual visitors would find this area of land remarkably unchanged, except for the removal of boundary fences to make the Greater Kruger Conservation area, part of the Great Limpopo Transfrontier park, which spans the borders of Mozambique and Zimbabwe.

The first game warden of the newly proclaimed Kruger National Park, and of the Sabie game reserve before that, was Colonel James Stevenson-Hamilton. A Scottish cavalry officer, Stevenson-Hamilton was renowned for his endless energy and dogged determination. This gave him the nickname 'Skukuza' and the administrative headquarters of the Kruger Park are named after him. A memorial to him can be found a short drive from Skukuza camp along the S22. In fact, there are many historical sites throughout the park, reminding us of the history of the area that dates back as far as the Stone Age, through the exploration of the lowveld in the early 19th century and on to other significant figures during the history of the park. Many of these sites are to be found within Skukuza camp and all are well worth taking in on your visit.

Local communities are playing an increasing role in Kruger forming partnerships with SANParks to operate conservancies within the boundaries of the park.

Climate

The Kruger Park's climate is affected by the seasonal variations in weather. Essentially, the Kruger Park has two seasons. The 'rainy season' summer months between November and April can be hot and humid, with temperatures exceeding 40°C, whilst the 'dry season' from May to October has warm days with cool nights. These seasonal changes can affect sightings as available water sources and daily temperatures often affect animal movements. Sparse vegetation during the winter months may make animals easier to spot and often at these times animals congregate where they can find water. Lush vegetation may make spotting harder in the summer months, but other special attractions more than compensate. For example, the early summer months of November and December are the start of the Impala lambing season and see the return of migratory birds. In the heat of the day during the summer months, many animals seek shade and barely move, whilst in the cooler winter months animals may be active throughout the day.

Clear blue skies are a feature of the climate in Kruger.

Month	Average daily min / °C	Average daily max / °C
January	18	34
February	18	33
March	18	33
April	13	28
May	13	28
June	9	26
July	9	26
August	12	28
September	12	28
October	16	32
November	16	32
December	18	34

Landscape and geology

Underlying rocks determine the types of plant that grow and consequently the diversity and abundance of animal and bird species that are found there. This is because, over time, the rock weathers, releasing nutrients that are essential for life. Generalising, much of the eastern half of the Kruger has underlying basalt. This gives rise to sweet, palatable grasses that provide nourishment for high game densities. The west of the Kruger sits on granite. This harder weathering rock produces less fertile soil. In these areas the valleys tend to have more palatable vegetation and this in turn leads to a greater abundance of grazers and their predators. There are also seven major river systems that flow through the park. River systems often attract higher densities of game.

Driving through Kruger you will notice that much of the park consists of gently undulating plains. Generally, the northern half of the park, above Olifants camp, is characterised by mopane veld, while the southern half is a varied mixture dominated by knobthorn, bush-willow and marula trees. Below Skukuza, some of the vegetation can be extremely dense and the area around Berg-en-Dal has more hills than the rest of the park.

Wildlife

Within these differing ecosystems, a wide variety of fauna and flora may be found. 147 species of mammal, 114 reptiles and 507 bird species complement the almost 2000 species of plants. You could expect to see over 50 of these mammal species and 100 bird species during your visit. You may be lucky enough to see several types of reptile, although snake sightings are generally rare. Many visitors are understandably keen to see the big five of Lion, Leopard, White or Black Rhinoceros, Elephant and Buffalo. However, appreciating the variety of other species on your game drive will enhance your visit further.

Giraffe are common and regularly spotted in the Kruger Park

1.2: Essential information.

How to book

South African National Parks operate the Kruger and it is through this organisation that bookings are made, either by telephoning or emailing central reservations or by booking online through the SANParks website.

Getting there

The Kruger Park is essentially a self-drive safari destination. The park is criss-crossed by a network of tarred and sand roads that are easy to navigate. South Africa has an excellent road network and this makes getting to the Kruger Park by car relatively easy, although you should remember that South Africa is a huge country and that distances can be large. Four airports serve the park. Kruger-Mpumalanga international airport has several daily flights to and from the area. It is situated close to White River, just north of the main town of Nelspruit and is approximately an hour's drive from the entrance gates to the park. Hoedspruit and Phalaborwa are the other airports outside the park, with Phalaborwa airport having the advantage of being alongside the park boundary. Skukuza airport has the advantage of being situated within the boundaries of the park, offering extremely efficient access to the south of the park. All airports are well served by car rental companies.

If you are staying outside of the park you have the alternative of paying a safari company to drive you to and within the Kruger Park.

Type of car

The Kruger Park has been designed to make travelling within its boundaries as easy as possible. All of the roads are well maintained and many are paved in tarmac. With this in mind, you don't need to break the bank and hire a 4x4 vehicle. All cars will be able to travel on the roads of Kruger and, on the whole, you will have the same viewing experience whatever car you choose to drive. Having said that, the grass in some parts of Kruger can grow to be very tall during the summer months and a higher sided vehicle may be an advantage at these times. In terms of photography, you will be at eye level with the animals in a sedan type vehicle and this should make for pleasing photographs. There are some roads in Kruger that, depending on the weather, you can book to drive along that take you away from the main tourist roads. These are currently only operational near Satara and a 4x4 vehicle is needed for these. There are also some low maintenance roads around Phalaborwa where a high clearance vehicle is recommended.

Kori bustards in early morning mist

Entering the park

Nine entrance gates allow you access to the park. Five of these are situated in the southernmost part, with the Paul Kruger gate being the closest to the main camp Skukuza. Opening times of these gates varies with season and can be different to the opening times of the main restcamps. You should pay close attention to these times as late entry to restcamps will result in a fine and entry to the park after gate closing time is forbidden. As you check into your first camp you will need to either pay a daily conservation fee or purchase a wild card. A wild card gives you unlimited access to certain South African national parks and may be a more economic option, depending on the length of your stay.

Month	Entrance gates		Camp gates	
	Open	Close	Open	Close
January	05:30	18:30	04:30	18:30
February	05:30	18:30	05:30	18:30
March	05:30	18:00	05:30	18:00
April	06:00	18:00	06:00	18:00
May	06:00	17:30	06:00	17:30
June	06:00	17:30	06:00	17:30
July	06:00	17:30	06:00	17:30
August	06:00	18:00	06:00	18:00
September	06:00	18:00	06:00	18:00
October	05:30	18:00	05:30	18:00
November	05:30	18:30	04:30	18:30
December	05:30	18:30	04:30	18:30

You must adhere to gate and camp opening and closing times.

Safety

By far the biggest risks posed to humans are the animals of the Kruger Park. Snakes, rats, mice, bats and other small mammals have been around in all the rest camps for many years. Snakes are rarely seen and avoid contact with humans where possible. If you do encounter one within a camp, keep your distance and contact reception. You may be far from medical help and bites could be fatal, so don't be tempted to deal with a snake yourself. You should always use a torch if walking around camp at night to be sure of what is on the path ahead of you. It is often interesting to have an ultraviolet torch as well, as these will show the scorpions hiding within the crack of trees. One of the biggest killers in Africa is malaria. Malaria is endemic to the Kruger Park. However, preventative management means that the risk is usually low. Most mosquitos do not carry malaria so being bitten does not mean that you will contract the disease. Anti-malarial prophylaxis is recommended, but avoiding being bitten is the best prevention. Cover exposed skin and use mosquito repellent, particularly at dusk and dawn when mosquitos are most active.

Tap water in the Kruger is safe to drink and bottled water is readily available. Keep some water with you in your car in case of emergencies. Food hygiene standards are good and you are unlikely to have any problems with food.

Crime is virtually non-existent in Kruger. However, you should still take the same precautions with your belongings, as you would do anywhere else in the world.

Alcohol is only permitted for overnight guests. You will need to show your accommodation booking to buy alcohol in the shops.

Before going out in the morning in search of animals you should make sure that you have put all foodstuffs securely away. Many camps issue warnings as monkeys and baboons have learnt to open fridge doors and cupboards and can become aggressive. Be aware of monkeys and baboons at picnic spots and get out points. These animals have become a pest in some places and are quick and adept at entering vehicles.

Be aware that carnivores can move more quickly than you realise and that windows should be closed if viewing them close to your vehicle.

Of the large animals it is elephants that perhaps pose the biggest risk to vehicles. You should follow these general rules when watching elephants:

Leave a good distance (50m+) between you and the elephants.

Do not drive off the road.

Plan your exit route. This can often be done by driving past the elephants before stopping to observe them.

Do not follow elephants.

Allow elephants the right of way.

Do not cut off an elephant's path.

Do not rev your engine.

Breeding herds: you should be careful of breeding herds with small calves. The matriarch and other herd members can become aggressive if calves feel threatened by your presence.

Musth bulls: Musth is a condition characterised by heightened levels of aggression. Keep your distance form musth bulls that can be identified by the secretions from temporal glands behind the eyes.

Give elephants plenty of space on the roads of Kruger.

Money matters

Cash is very important for all travellers to the Kruger Park. Whilst many of the shops and restaurants in larger camps will accept credit and debit cards, the fuel stations will only accept cash for your petrol or diesel purchases. There are ATM's at Skukuza, Letaba and Shingwedzi.

Fuel and garages

All of the main rest camps have a garage where you can fill up your vehicle with both petrol and diesel. Whilst these garages may be able to help with any vehicle problems, it is at Skukuza where you will find the garage with the best facilities for repairing any vehicle problems.

Electricity

Electricity is supplied to all of the main rest camps and your accommodation will have several accessible plug sockets. It is worth remembering that overseas visitors will need an adaptor to fit South African plug sockets. The availability of electricity in other rest camps is variable.

What to pack

What you need to bring with you to the Kruger Park will very much depend on your choice of accommodation and activities. If you are camping then you will need at least a tent, mattress, sleeping bags, cooking and eating utensils and washing up gear. A cooler box would also be good and if you wish to use the caravan electricity points you will need an extension cable and adaptor. If you are staying in any other kind of accommodation, most of what you need will be provided for you, including bedding, towels and soap. Not all units include cooking utensils, however, so you should check this at the point of booking.

As most days are at least pleasantly warm all year round, you should pack clothes that will be comfortable in this heat and include a hat, sunglasses and sunscreen. A swimming costume will be needed if you plan on making use of the many swimming pools at the main rest camps. At night the temperature can be surprisingly low, especially during the winter months, so you will also need to pack something warm. Long sleeves and trousers will help avoid mosquito bites during the cooler hours of dawn and dusk. If you are planning on a night or sunset drive you will need warm clothing as these are in open vehicles and you can become cold if you are unprepared.

Binoculars are vital equipment for all visitors. Ideally, everyone should have his or her own binoculars, as it can be frustrating having to share.

Many visitors will want to record the sightings that they see on a video or camera. It is important to ensure that you have the best optical zoom lens possible, with the longest reach you can afford, and lots and lots of memory cards.

As you are in the African bush and potentially far from help, a basic first aid kit with antihistamine, plasters, paracetamol and any other regular medication is recommended.

Don't forget to pack your map book, animal and bird guides. If you don't have them, these can be purchased at entrance gates and shops in the main camps.

Disabled visitors

Disabled visitors are well catered for within the park. People with mobility challenges make frequent use of the park and are able to access most places, including all of the main camps and picnic sites. Accommodation in each of the main camps caters for people with mobility challenges. It is advisable to check that your chosen accommodation meets your requirements at the time of booking.

Shopping

All main rest camps have a shop where you can buy groceries, clothes and souvenirs. Availability of groceries can be variable and is better in the south of the park. However, you will always be able to find plenty of food if you wish to prepare your own meals. Clothes and souvenirs can be expensive and are of the same kind of goods that you can buy in Johannesburg airport.

Section two: Maps of the Kruger park.

2.1 Park outline map

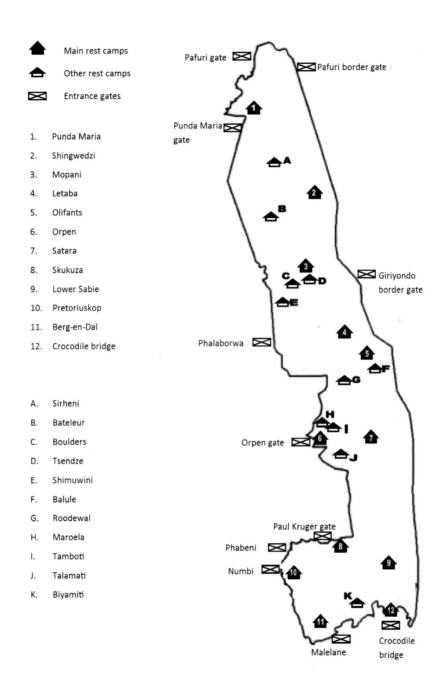

Legend:

- 🏠 Main rest camps
- 🏠 Other rest camps
- ✉ Entrance gates

1. Punda Maria
2. Shingwedzi
3. Mopani
4. Letaba
5. Olifants
6. Orpen
7. Satara
8. Skukuza
9. Lower Sabie
10. Pretoriuskop
11. Berg-en-Dal
12. Crocodile bridge

A. Sirheni
B. Bateleur
C. Boulders
D. Tsendze
E. Shimuwini
F. Balule
G. Roodewal
H. Maroela
I. Tamboti
J. Talamati
K. Biyamiti

2.2 Kruger Park Road map key

Key to maps

 Main rest camp

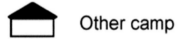 Other camp

 Picnic spot

 Entrance gate

(W) Waterhole or dam

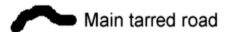 Main tarred road

Sand or gravel road

River

Bird hide

Get out point (at your own risk)

2.3 The far south of Kruger

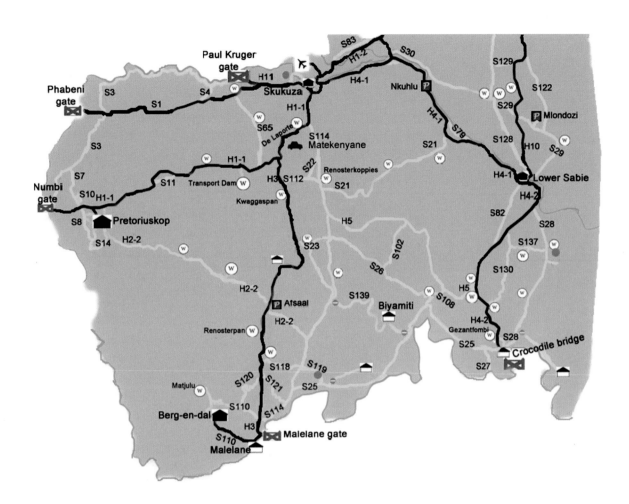

2.4 Southern central Kruger: from Skukuza to Satara.

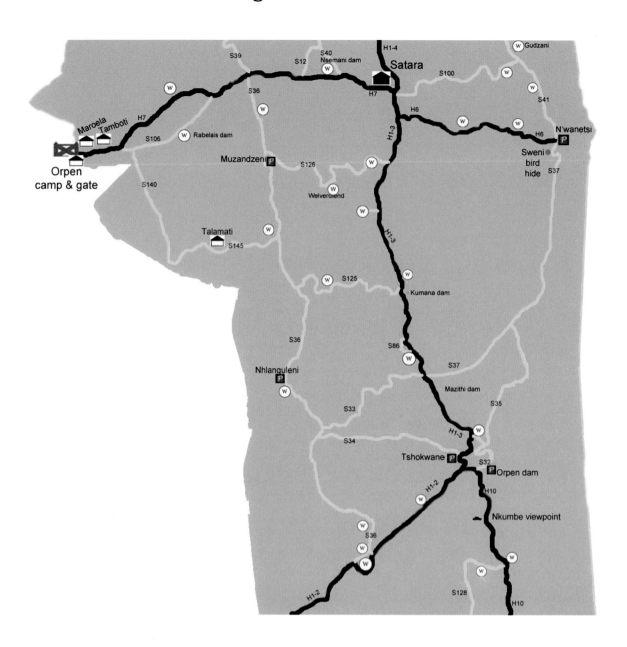

2.5 Central Kruger: from Satara to Letaba.

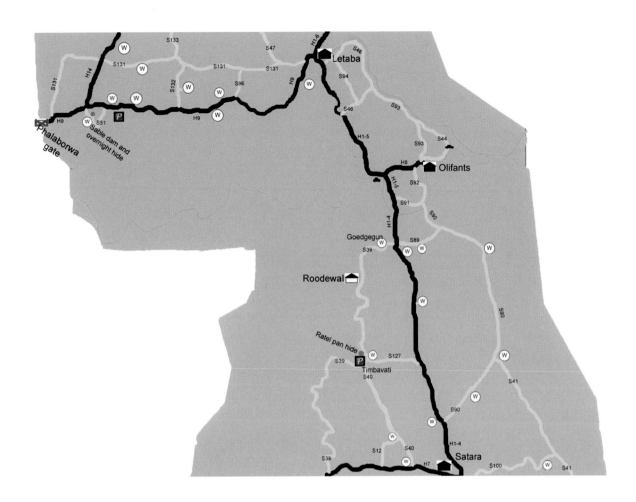

2.6 Northern Kruger: from Letaba to Shingwedzi.

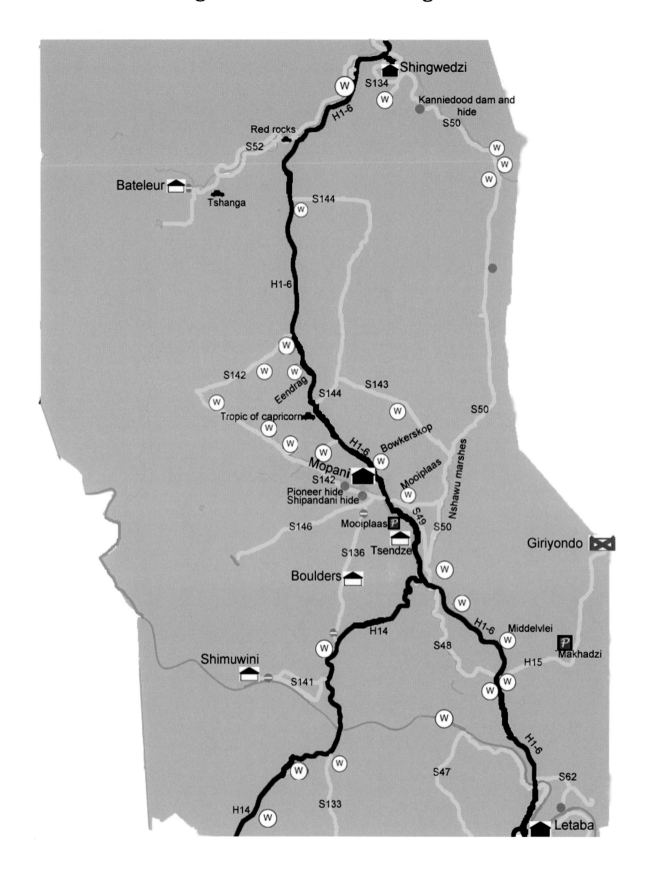

2.7 Far north of Kruger: from Shingwedzi to Pafuri.

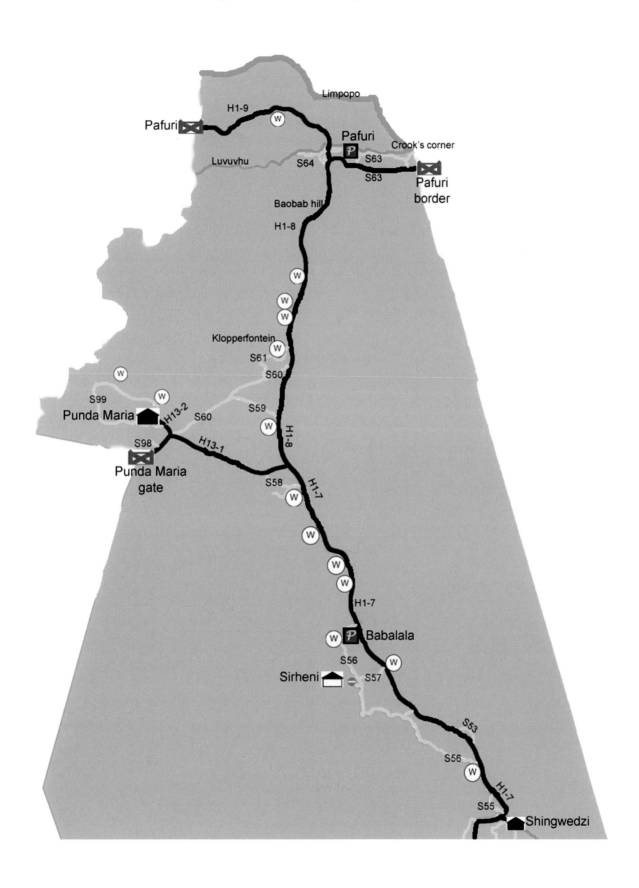

Section three: Camp guides

Within the Kruger National Park there are twenty-six camps to stay in. These comprise main camps, bushveld camps, bush lodges, overnight hides and camping sites. Each camp and each type of accommodation has its own unique atmosphere. Accommodation ranges from your own campsite to large guesthouses that will accommodate large groups. There are also nine luxury concessions, run by and for the local communities surrounding the park.

When booking accommodation you should consider that it can take a long time to cover relatively short distances. It is inadvisable to book accommodation for subsequent nights in camps that are a long distance apart. Each region of the park also has its own distinct feel and you should also take this into account when deciding upon which camps you would like to stay in. Below the Sabie River, game is plentiful and you should be rewarded with frequent animal sightings. However, this part of the park is also the busiest in terms of people, so sightings can become congested at peak times. In central Kruger, the open plains provide excellent grazing this in turn attracts large predator numbers. Further north, game densities are lower and there are fewer visitors. Whilst you may have fewer sightings, these sightings will be more special and intimate. Many return visitors to the Kruger Park savour the more peaceful, traditional bush feel of northern Kruger.

Accommodation is available to book eleven months in advance. Popular camps, such as Lower Sabie, and peak times such as the public school holidays, will get booked up very quickly.

The old world charm of Punda Maria

3.1 Below the Sabie river.

Berg-en-Dal and Malelane

Situated in the far southwest of the park and set in a mountainous environment close to Malelane gate, Berg-en-Dal overlooks a dam in the seasonal Matjulu spruit where animals come to drink. A large and spacious camp, there is accommodation within campsites, bungalows, family cottages and guesthouses. The camp has a swimming pool, café, launderette, fuel, a large shop and a restaurant. Uniquely, Berg-en-dal has a braille trail and a 'rhino trail' to guide you on a walk through the natural vegetation inside the camp fence. The camp has been well designed and many trees can be found within the camp boundaries. You will not have to leave camp to enjoy the variety of bird species that are attracted to these trees and other vegetation.

Malelane is uniquely placed on the boundary of the park, overlooking the Crocodile River. A small, intimate camp, there are no facilities for the 19 guests. Check-in is at Berg-en-Dal.

Biyamiti

This popular bush camp is one of my favourite camps. Situated on the banks of the Mbiyamiti River, guests here enjoy 21km of a superb game-viewing road that is only open to overnight guests and where all of the larger mammals are regularly seen. There are fifteen cottages but no other facilities such as a shop, restaurant or fuel so visitors must be self-sufficient.

Crocodile Bridge

Sharing its name with the entrance gate and river where it is located in the south east of the park, Crocodile Bridge is a smaller camp with only 20 huts, eight safari tents and a small number of campsites. This small but picturesque camp has few facilities apart from a shop and fuel station, but lies in a renowned game viewing area.

Lower Sabie

Another of my favourite camps, Lower Sabie is one of the most popular camps within the park and often gets fully booked many months in advance. This is due to its magnificent location on the Sabie River, the superb game viewing area around the camp and the family friendly green lawns shaded by large trees. Sunset dam, a favourite place to sit and watch the coming and going of animals, is less than 1km from the camp. Accommodation is in campsites, huts, bungalows, guest cottages, safari tents and a guesthouse. The camp has a fuel station and a large shop whilst a café and restaurant overlook the river.

Pretoriuskop

The oldest rest camp in the Kruger Park, there are often Impala, Warthog and Guinea fowl around your accommodation in Pretoriuskop. Accommodation is in campsites, huts, bungalows, guest cottages, family cottages and a guesthouse. As with other main camps, Pretoriuskop has good facilities including a large shop, fuel station, café and restaurant.

Skukuza

Skukuza is the administrative headquarters of the park and is large and busy. It is close to a main entrance gate (Paul Kruger gate) and easily accessible from Kruger-Mpumalanga airport and Skukuza airport. Here you will find amenities such as a bank and post office as well as many important historical sites such as a library and dog cemetery. There is also a fuel station, two restaurants, a large shop and a swimming pool. The camp itself is situated on a beautiful stretch of the Sabie River, overlooking the old Selati train bridge. On one occasion at dusk I watched a large male leopard patrol the riverbed from just outside the restaurant. Accommodation is in campsites, huts, bungalows, guest cottages, safari tents and guesthouses, with many enjoying a view over the river. A large day visitor's area can be found adjacent to the camp.

3.2 Central Kruger

Olifants with Balule

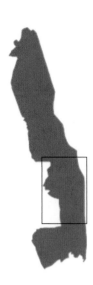

Olifants sits high on a cliff with sensational views of the Olifants river below and the bush beyond and it is for this reason that it is on my list of favourite camps. Accommodation here is in either bungalows or one of the two guesthouses. There are no camping facilities – these are found at the satellite camp Balule. Olifants camp benefits from the usual facilities, including a restaurant with fabulous views and a swimming pool.

Balule is situated 4km from Olifants, on the southern banks of the river. This most basic of camps has no electricity and only the most basic of facilities for campers and caravanning people. There are also six basic huts. Consequently, Balule is one of the best places in the park to experience the night sky without any light pollution. You must report to one of the nearby main rest camps to check in to Balule.

The view from Olifants camp.

Orpen with Maroela and Tamboti

Orpen camp is situated in a central position on the western boundary of the park and couples as an entrance gate. There is a small shop and a swimming pool but no restaurant. Guests may stay in one of the bungalows or guest cottages. Caravans and camping can be found 2km away, along the Timbavati River at Maroela camp. There is a rustic viewing platform overlooking the river at Maroela but no other facilities. You must check in at Orpen if you are staying here or at Tamboti, a camp consisting of safari tent accommodation. A bird hide here offers you a chance to take in the surroundings.

Hyena by the roadside

Roodewal

Roodewal enjoys a secluded location on the banks of the Timbavati River between Satara and Olifants camps. This very small camp can be booked for one group only and therefore offers a very private experience. There is a viewing platform to enjoy sightings along the riverbed. The only facilities are for self-catering and electricity is limited.

Satara

A busy camp in the heart of the park, surrounded by prime game viewing habitat, Satara offers all the usual amenities that you would associate with a larger camp. The bungalows at Satara are mainly arranged in circles with shady lawns and a swimming pool with children's playground making this camp ideal for children. Guests can also camp or stay in one of the guesthouses. A day visitor's area is found along the fence at the front of camp. Satara is a camp that I always try to stay in, as it is renowned for the high proportion of cat sightings on the roads that radiate through the fertile plains surrounding camp.

The shop and restaurant area at Satara camp.

Talamati

Situated in a large open valley in a remote part of the central region, Talamati offers privacy amongst its fifteen cottages. There are no facilities here and guests are required to self cater.

3.3 Northern Kruger

Bateleur

Named after the majestic Bateleur eagle, this bushveld camp is the oldest and also the smallest of its type. A quiet atmosphere greets the guests staying within the seven self-catering cottages. There is a bird hide from which to watch wildlife coming to a small waterhole and two dams along roads reserved for residents only.

Boulders

This bush lodge is embedded within the rocky outcrops that are found in this area. Close to Mopani camp, wooden walkways link the accommodation units that are built on stilts and must be booked by a single party. There are no facilities here and guests are required to be self-sufficient.

Mopani with Tsendze

Named after the dominant mopane vegetation in the surrounding area, Mopani overlooks the large and impressive Pioneer dam. Guests can stay in a variety of bungalows and guesthouses that are set within natural bush surroundings. As a main camp, Mopani offers the usual facilities including fuel, a shop, swimming pool and restaurant. Camping can be found at nearby Tsendze, a camping and caravan only camp with no electricity.

Letaba

Letaba rest camp is situated on a sweeping bend of the sandy Letaba River. Guests can stay in a variety of accommodation including campsites, bungalows and guesthouses. All the usual facilities of a main rest camp can be found here, including fuel, a shop, swimming pool and restaurant. This camp is a perfect base to look for many of the large elephants within the park. An elephant hall within camp celebrates the life of elephants and those elephants of the past with huge tusks that came to be known as 'the magnificent seven'.

The elephant hall, Letaba

Punda Maria

Situated in the northernmost part of the park, Punda Maria is a quiet main camp with a hide that overlooks a waterhole. Camping, safari tents and bungalow accommodation is available. As a main camp, Punda Maria offers the usual amenities including fuel, a shop, swimming pool and restaurant.

Shimuwini

Fifteen cottages line the bank of the Letaba River in this bushveld camp where guests are required to be self-sufficient. There are many ancient baobab trees visible from the camp and there is a small road network that is only accessible to overnight guests.

Shingwedzi

Shingwedzi lies along the river of the same name in prime elephant habitat. Guests can stay in a variety of accommodation including camping, safari tents, bungalows and a guesthouse. This camp has a peaceful charm although still has the same facilities that you would expect to find in a main camp including fuel, a shop, swimming pool and restaurant. The tranquil atmosphere makes Shingwedzi a favourite.

Typical accommodation at Shingwedzi

Sirheni

Alongside the Sirheni dam in the northern Kruger lies Sirheni, a small, peaceful bushveld camp. Two bird hides overlook a small dam here. Guests at this camp will need to be self-sufficient as there is no facilities other than those found within the cottages.

Shipandani and Sable hides

Bird hides by day, these hides accommodate between two and nine guests for a unique self-catering experience away from any other visitors. Guests report to Mopani (Shipandani) or Phalaborwa gate (Sable) to pick up the required keys.

A view of Shipandani hide

Section four: while you are there.

4.1 Distances between main rest camps and entrance gates

You should plan to be driving around 25 to 30 kph whilst in the park. At these speeds you should cover 100km in three and a half to four hours. You will also need to factor in time spent game viewing and time stopped at picnic sites and get out points.

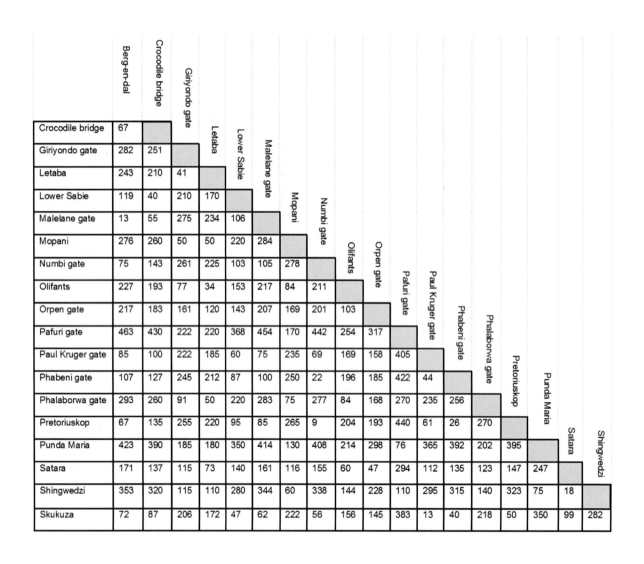

	Berg-en-dal	Crocodile bridge	Giriyondo gate	Letaba	Lower Sabie	Malelane gate	Mopani	Numbi gate	Olifants	Orpen gate	Pafuri gate	Paul Kruger gate	Phabeni gate	Phalaborwa gate	Pretoriuskop	Punda Maria	Satara	Shingwedzi
Crocodile bridge	67																	
Giriyondo gate	282	251																
Letaba	243	210	41															
Lower Sabie	119	40	210	170														
Malelane gate	13	55	275	234	106													
Mopani	276	260	50	50	220	284												
Numbi gate	75	143	261	225	103	105	278											
Olifants	227	193	77	34	153	217	84	211										
Orpen gate	217	183	161	120	143	207	169	201	103									
Pafuri gate	463	430	222	220	368	454	170	442	254	317								
Paul Kruger gate	85	100	222	185	60	75	235	69	169	158	405							
Phabeni gate	107	127	245	212	87	100	250	22	196	185	422	44						
Phalaborwa gate	293	260	91	50	220	283	75	277	84	168	270	235	256					
Pretoriuskop	67	135	255	220	95	85	265	9	204	193	440	61	26	270				
Punda Maria	423	390	185	180	350	414	130	408	214	298	76	365	392	202	395			
Satara	171	137	115	73	140	161	116	155	60	47	294	112	135	123	147	247		
Shingwedzi	353	320	115	110	280	344	60	338	144	228	110	295	315	140	323	75	18	
Skukuza	72	87	206	172	47	62	222	56	156	145	383	13	40	218	50	350	99	282

4.2 Camp facilities

	Petrol	Day visitor facilities	Shop	Toilet facilities	Swimming pool	Restaurant	Electricity	Pitch your own Camping / caravans	Conference facilities	Cultural sites	Refrigeration	KNP emergency road service
Balule				Y				Y				
Bateleur				Y			Y		Y		Y	
Berg-en-dal	Y	Y	Y	Y	Y	Y	Y	Y	Y	Y	Y	Y
Biyamiti				Y			Y				Y	
Boulders				Y							Y	
Crocodile bridge	Y	Y	Y	Y				Y			Y	
Letaba	Y	Y	Y	Y	Y	Y	Y	Y	Y	Y	Y	Y
Lower Sabie	Y	Y	Y	Y	Y	Y	Y	Y			Y	Y
Malelane camp				Y				Y			Y	
Maroela				Y				Y			Y	
Mopani	Y	Y	Y	Y	Y	Y	Y		Y		Y	Y
Olifants	Y	Y	Y	Y	Y	Y	Y				Y	Y
Orpen	Y	Y	Y	Y	Y	Y	Y				Y	
Pretoriuskop	Y	Y	Y	Y	Y	Y	Y	Y			Y	Y
Punda Maria	Y	Y	Y	Y	Y	Y	Y	Y			Y	
Roodewal				Y							Y	
Satara	Y	Y	Y	Y	Y	Y	Y	Y			Y	Y
Shingwedzi	Y	Y	Y	Y	Y	Y	Y	Y	Y		Y	Y
Sirheni				Y			Y				Y	
Skukuza	Y	Y	Y	Y	Y	Y	Y	Y	Y	Y	Y	Y
Talamati				Y			Y				Y	
Tamboti				Y							Y	
Tsendze				Y							Y	

4.3: Kruger Park Rules.

Upon entering the park you will be given a leaflet containing the main rules and regulations. The main rules are listed here.

Visitors enter at their own risk.

All firearms must be declared at entrance gates.

Gate times must be strictly adhered to.

Guests are only allowed to stay at booked and recognized overnight facilities and must report to the relevant reception before occupying accommodation or camping.

All accommodation and camping sites may be occupied from 14:00 on day of arrival and must be vacated by 10:00 on the day of departure.

Do not exceed the speed limit – 50kph on tar roads and 40kph on gravel roads. Speed traps operate within the park.

The general rules of the road apply within the Kruger Park.

Stay on designated roads: off-road driving is prohibited.

Do not protrude from your vehicle and remain in your vehicle unless at a designated get out point.

The consumption of alcohol in public areas is prohibited. Day visitors are prohibited from entering Kruger National Park with any alcohol in their vehicles.

Feeding animals is prohibited and will lead to the death of these animals as they become dangerous to humans.

No pets are allowed and no fauna or flora may be removed from the park.

No littering.

The park is a noise free zone.

4.4: Game drives.

For most visitors, the main reason for visiting the Kruger Park is to spot animals and birds. Camp gates are open for around twelve hours a day and you will want to maximise your time driving on the roads of Kruger to see as many animals and birds as possible. Whilst it is undoubtedly true that most of your sightings will be on the roads, it may be worth taking into account the camp you are staying in, the season and the age of people in your group. Some camps, such as Letaba, are great for spending some time in and watching the resident animals and birds or life in the river. In the summer months, many animals seek shade and barely move from mid morning to mid afternoon and you may find it better to spend this time in camp. Children rarely like to spend long hours in a car, and many camps offer opportunities for stretching legs, playing games on grassy lawns and most camps now have swimming pools.

Although many visitors to the park are eager to see the 'big five', it is far more rewarding to appreciate all that Kruger has to offer. By stopping to watch and listen you can become more attuned to the environment and use these clues to see some of the larger animals. I can also think of several times where I have stopped to watch something commonplace and been rewarded with a spectacular sighting, including the time spent watching a giraffe which led to an incredible sighting of a leopard mother and her two cubs crossing the road. I was the only car who had stopped to watch the giraffe and consequently had the leopard sighting all to myself for a considerable time.

Game viewing is a pleasurable experience and you should follow some simple viewing etiquette to ensure that all tourists can share your sightings with you in an enjoyable way for everyone. Below are some tips to follow so that everyone can enjoy the sightings. These could be summarised by having respect for the environment and respect and consideration for other visitors.

It is always pleasant to wave to and talk about your sightings with visitors in other vehicles. Don't use sightings apps. SANParks do not support the use of these applications. Instead, talk to other visitors and use the sightings boards that are located in camps and some picnic sites.

Drive slowly. Speed limits are 50kph on tar roads and 40kph on all other roads. However, even these speeds making game viewing difficult. Try to stick to around 25-30kph. This will make game viewing easier whilst still allowing you to cover some ground.
When you spot something that you want to watch, pull over to the side of the road that the sighting is on, paying careful attention not to block the road.

Keep your distance, especially from big animals, and do not drive off the road surface.

Approach game slowly. For most animals, you can switch your engine off if the animals are settled in your presence. Around elephants it is wise to leave your engine running in most instances.

If you are approaching a stationary vehicle, slow down so that you do not scare off what they are looking at.

Keep noise to a minimum. This includes not using your mobile phone.

Do not be tempted to feed the animals. This will invariably seal their death sentence as they will become too habituated to humans and may become aggressive.

Stay within your vehicle. This includes not having arms protruding from your window. Not only will this ensure your safety, animals will run off if parts of your body break the silhouette of your car.

Many animals are easily visible on or close to the roads in Kruger.

Animal census

This table gives an approximate idea of the number of these common animals and some of the rare animals within the Kruger Park, using the most up to date information (source: www.sanparks.org).

Animal name	Approximate number
Lion	1,620 – 1,750
Leopard	1,000
Cheetah	120
Wild dog	120
Spotted hyena	5340
Elephant	13,750
Burchell's Zebra	23,700 – 35,300
Hippopotamus	3,100
Warthog	3,100 – 5,700
Giraffe	6,800 – 10,300
Buffalo	37,130
Eland	460
Roan antelope	90
Sable antelope	290
Greater Kudu	11,200 – 17,300
Nyala	+300
Waterbuck	3,100 – 7,800
Reedbuck	300
Blue wildebeest	6,400 – 13,100
Tsessebe	220
Impala	132,300 -176,400
Crocodile	4420

Best spotting tips

The most consistently productive times of the day for game viewing are the early morning and late afternoon.

Rivers and waterholes attract birds and animals throughout the day, but especially in the afternoon when many of the larger herbivores appear to drink.

Drive slowly – around 25 to 30 kilometres per hour is best. You will see more, disturb fewer animals with sudden braking and still be able to cover sufficient ground.

Use sightings boards wisely. Each camp has a board where visitors can 'mark' their sightings for the today. This might help you plan your drives, although you should bear in mind that many sightings are fleeting and you cannot guarantee the accuracy of information.

Game viewing doesn't stop when the sun sets. Book yourself onto a sunset or night drive, or use a torch to view the nocturnal visitors within camp or those that patrol the perimeter fence.

Waterholes are a great place to find wildlife.

4.5: Game viewing routes.

With game viewing it is very much the case of being in the right place at the right time. However, you can vastly increase your chances of successful game drives by knowing something about the animals that you wish to see. You should aim to leave camp when the gates open. Nocturnal animals, including the big predators, may still be active; it is not unusual to find lions on the road early in a morning. Most animals are also more active in this cooler period of the day. In the summer months, many animals find shade and rest through the hottest parts of the day. However, in the winter months, with cooler days, animals may stay active throughout the daylight hours. All animals need water and it is often from mid morning that they start to make their way to water holes and rivers for a drink. As dusk approaches, nocturnal animals may once again make an appearance as they begin their activities.

In the next section I have outlined some productive game viewing routes. These are based on personal experience and by talking to other guests and park staff. However, remember that all roads have the potential to offer great sightings so do not discount completely roads that are listed, as you may still be lucky. As a general rule, road numbers prefixed with an 'H' are paved and those roads prefixed with an 'S' are gravel. The exceptions are the H2-2, H5 and H15, which are gravel roads and the S1, S63 and S110, which are tar roads. Tarred roads often carry heavier traffic but the habituated animals close to these roads often compensate this. Sand or gravel roads can become dusty and corrugated and may even be temporarily closed after heavy rain but often fewer vehicles use these roads.

How to choose roads and plan your route.

When choosing your route through Kruger, consult your maps carefully. You should study the map, deciding if you are doing a shorter morning or afternoon drive or a longer day drive. Will you be returning to the same camp or moving camps? When you have decided, look for opportunities to stretch your legs and top up with food and drink. Look at the recommended routes for each area and identify the places where animals may come to drink. As already outlined, you should plan to drive at 25 to 30 kmh. At this speed you will cover around 100km in four hours. A typical morning drive will usually take around four hours; an afternoon drive may be shorter. You should not plan to drive more than 250km in a day.

Around Berg-en-dal

A picturesque, hilly environment surrounds Berg-en-dal and the area is one of the most diverse in terms of flora. White rhino are common around this camp and you should be on the lookout for them, although game viewing in the immediate area around the camp can be unpredictable. The drive from camp along the S110 to Matjulu water hole is worth doing as a variety of animals sometimes appear here and elephant are common. The H3 offers good sightings but this road can be busy with a lot of traffic going towards and from Malelane gate. Leopards are reported frequently in the few kilometres close to Malelane gate and wild dog appear to be common around this area too. Afsaal picnic site lies along this road and is a great place to stop at any time of the day. Just before Afsaal the terrain opens out and you can often spot several species feeding on the grass here. Between Malelane gate and Afsaal, four gravel roads take you east towards Crocodile Bridge. All offer good chances of seeing game, with the most southern of these, the S114/S25, being the most productive personally. The pleasant riverine habitat gives you a good chance of spotting predators such as lion. The S25 is also the road where I have had most luck with black rhino sightings.

Buffalo, Berg-en-dal area

Morning drive

Take the tarred S110 from camp to the H3. The S110 traverses mountain bushveld. Game densities are generally low, but there are frequent elephant sightings and you may expect to see kudu and giraffe. Follow the H3 north to Afsaal picnic site where you may want a brief stop. The entire H3 can be very productive. Both leopard and wild dog are seen relatively frequently along this route. Look into the riverbed as you cross the Mhlambane river. Along the way, Renosterpan may be worth the short detour as many animals utilise this drinking place regularly. Carry on north, and then take the S113 to the east to meet up with the S23. Follow this meandering road along the seasonal Biyamiti river. Animal sightings are regular and lion and leopard can be spotted along this route. As the road joins to the S114 you will find the Biyamiti weir. This is a magical place where you are at eye level with the water in the weir. Bird life abounds and you may happen upon a variety of animals that have come to quench their thirst. From here, follow the S114 south. This road offers reasonable chances of spotting browsers and predator sightings are fairly common. Follow the S114 until it meets the H3 and return to camp.

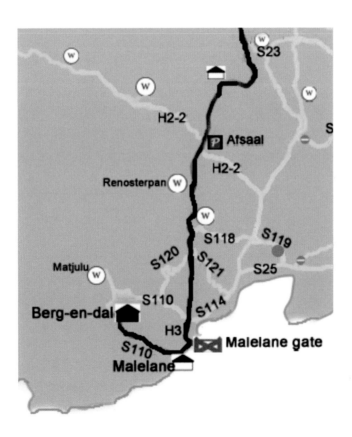

Further afield

From Berg-en-dal it is an easy day drive to Pretoriuskop and Skukuza camps and back. It is also possible to visit Lower Sabie but this is a longer trip.

To get to Pretoriuskop, follow the H3 to Afsaal then take the H2-2. This 44km road has many historical sites from its time as part of a transport route in the nineteenth century. Many of the incidents from 'Jock of the bushveld' by Percy Fitzpatrick occurred along this route. Along this route is Ship Mountain, named as it resembles the hull of an upturned ship. The road itself is better for browsers than grazers and you may see kudu, giraffe, impala and elephant. Closer to Pretoriuskop your chances of spotting white rhino increase. To return to Berg-en-dal, take the H1-1 to the east and meet up with the H3 that you can follow in a southerly direction. Sightings can be sparse along the H1-1 but all of the big five are present. Look out for klipspringers around the Napi boulders area and in the outcrops at the junction of the H1-1 and H3. Lion often utilise these outcrops for nursing and protecting cubs. Transport dam along the H1-1 is often a busy watering spot for animals and birds alike. Following the H3 southwards, the road passes Kwaggaspan. Waterbuck and elephant are seen regularly and many grazers favour this area, bringing with them predators such as lion.

Following the H3 northwards from Berg-en-dal you will lead you to Skukuza. Beyond the intersection with the H1-1, this road soon passes Matekenyane, a granite outcrop where you can get out and survey the surrounding bush. Although the bush can be thick in places, the H1-1 towards Skukuza can provide many interesting sightings. To return to Skukuza take the S114. Dense thorn thickets give way to mixed bushwillow and sightings become more prolific. Renosterkoppies waterhole often attracts game from the immediate vicinity, including elephant, rhino and buffalo. Lion are often sighted here too and wild dog can be seen along this route.

Lower Sabie is along days drive from Berg-en-dal. The best route to take is the S114, branching onto the S25 after eight kilometres. This road can often carry higher volumes of traffic and many parts are badly corrugated. However, the road travels next to the Crocodile river for sections and passes through a variety of ecozones. Consequently a great variety of animal and plant life may be found here. You have a good chance of seeing almost anything along this route; elephant and giraffe are common. Take the S108 and H5 to meet up with the H4-2 towards Lower Sabie. This productive road consistently offers good sightings. The ubiquitous Impala are common and you can expect to see a variety of grazers such as zebra and wildebeest and browsers such as kudu. Birding is good along this route, especially as your reach the Sabie river, and your chances of seeing all of the big five are high. After a well-earned rest at Lower Sabie, take the H4-1 towards Skukuza. This is an outstanding road at any time of day; animals cross this road as they move towards and from the river to drink. Leopard and lion sightings are frequent. You should expect to encounter elephant along this route. You can continue along the H4-1 all the way to Skukuza or take the S21 to shorten the distance. The vegetation gradually changes along this route and it is a pleasing drive. Impala, warthog, giraffe and kudu are abundant but this road can be a bit hit and miss for other species. However, there are many magnificent tree specimens along this route and birding is good. At Renosterkoppies, take the S112 to join up with the H3 or use the S114 to return to Berg-en-dal.

Around Crocodile bridge

As an entrance gate to the southeastern region and being close to the popular camp Lower Sabie, the H4-2 carries a lot of traffic. For this reason it is advisable to travel on this road early in the morning if possible. However, you have excellent chances of spotting all of the big five animals along this route. To the west, the S25 heads towards Berg-en-dal along the Crocodile River. This is another excellent route and with high chances of spotting all of the big five animals. Lion are regularly seen along the first part of this route. A short road, the S27 leads to the 'Hippo pools' get out point. From mid morning to mid afternoon a ranger is on hand to escort you to the river to view the wildlife, including hippos and crocodiles. The S139 is a private road for guests staying at Biyamiti camp. At the far end this road joins with the S114 at the Biyamiti weir. All guests can access this part of the park where your vehicle goes below the height of the water above it, giving you an eye level view of crocodiles, hippos and other game that are coming for a drink. To the east of Crocodile Bridge, the S28 traverses open plains. Cheetah are a common sight along this road and your chances of spotting lion and the other members of the big five animals are also high.

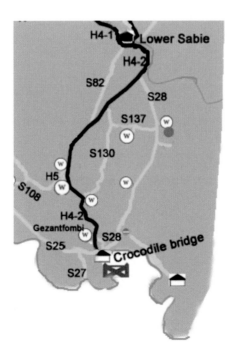

Morning drive

Guests staying at Crocodile Bridge are likely to be in transit into or out of the park. For a morning drive I would suggest taking the H4-2 to Lower Sabie. Predator sightings are common along this route and I have had my best wild dog sighting some four kilometres from camp. The area around the Gezantfombi dam often has lots of wild life. Lion can often be spotted here and may sometimes be found on the dam wall when water levels are lower. The whole route through to Lower Sabie camp can be prolific and you may spend much more time driving this route than you expect. Stop at camp to enjoy the view from the deck, before returning to Crocodile bridge on the S28. This road offers some of the best chances in the park of spotting Cheetah. The vegetation along this road is quite open. Zebra and white rhino are common. Look out for lion, hyena and black backed jackal.

Further afield

Beg-en-dal can be reached by using the S25. It is possible to get to Skukuza and back in a day trip. To do this, follow the H4-2 and H4-1 to get to Skukuza. As describe previously, both the H4-2 and H4-1 are exceptional roads where you will have numerous sightings. To return to Crocodile bridge from Skukuza you could do worse than to retrace your steps. Alternatively, take the H4-1 towards Lower Sabie. At the bridge across the Sabie river (H12), cross the bridge and turn left onto the S30. This is a superb dirt road; the first few kilometres that travel alongside the river are home to many animals. It is fairly common to see predators such as lion and wild dog around this area. Take as many of the loops down to the riverside as you have time for as they all offer something rewarding. Bushbuck are common and Nyala may be encountered. Elephant and buffalo regularly cross the road to visit the river. As the road moves away from the river the vegetation opens out, making the ideal habitat for lion and cheetah. Follow the S128 back towards Lower Sabie, crossing the low water bridge on the H10. Here you will spot crocodile, hippo and many water birds. Return to Crocodile bridge along the H4-2.

Wild dog near

Crocodile bridge

Around Pretoriuskop

Tall grass characterises the areas surrounding Pretoriuskop camp and this has made game viewing difficult for me in the past. The high rainfall experienced in this part of the park in the summer months is to blame. However, concentrations of game around camp seem high and I have had some exceptional sightings, including a pack of wild dog and a large pride of lions in the first kilometre from the camp gates. A network of sand roads surrounds the camp. Browsers such as kudu are common and I have seen a pleasing number of buffalo here too. The H2-2, leading to Afsaal, is a picturesque road. This 'Voortrekker road' passes many historical sights from the era of transport wagons, including the birthplace of the main character in `Jock of the bushveld'. I find the H1-1 to be slow in terms of sightings but have, over the years, seen all of the big five here. Transport dam is just off this road and is the site of the famous 'Battle of Kruger' video clip.

Morning drive

If you wish to return to Pretoriuskop for breakfast then I would recommend the network of gravel roads around camp. The S8, S14 and S20 can offer some surprising sightings but in general it is giraffe, impala and kudu that dominate. Following the H1-1 towards Numbi gate you can also take some other gravel loops. The S10 loops around the huge boulders of Shabeni hill. This is a natural place to look for klipspringers and both leopard and lion favour this rocky outcrop. The S7 and S3 via Mestel dam often have high grass obscuring your view, but elephant and white rhino are common. Mestel dam often attracts a variety of game.

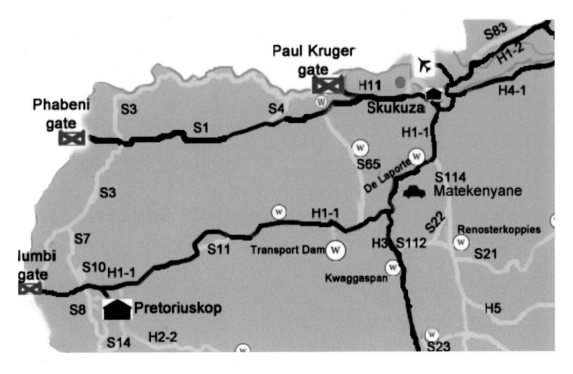

Further afield

Skukuza is not far away and can be accessed via the S3 and S1 or the H1-1. Of these I prefer the S1. Both roads can be busy due to their proximity to entrance gates. The lightly undulating landscape of the S1 often offers up sightings of zebra, buffalo and giraffe. Wild dog frequent this road and lion are regularly reported. Close to the intersection of the H11 is a heavily utilised hyena den and sightings of this predator are frequent. You could also cross the S1 and continue on the S3. Meandering along the river, this road shows signs of white rhino activity. Elephant are often encountered here too. In fact this road is one of my favourites as, despite the occasional glimpses of life beyond the park, this road is very scenic and you feel that almost anything is around the next corner. Bird life along the river is also prolific. Return to camp along any of the routes. A worthwhile detour in this area is the S65. Activity on this road is plentiful and some of the larger herds in the area can be found here. Lion and leopard sightings are frequent. The N'waswitshaka waterhole attracts a variety of species all through the day.

Baboon.

Around Skukuza

As the headquarters of the park and the largest camp, the roads around Skukuza can be very busy. However, you can often find surprisingly quiet sightings along the gravel roads in the area. Game sightings around this camp are excellent along many of the routes. One of my favourite tar roads, the H4-1 along the Sabie river, is teeming with game and I have had regular sightings of lion, leopard and the rest of the big five animals along this route. However, I prefer to go along the H1-2 and H12 for the first part of this journey. I have had incredible success with lion here in the early morning and I enjoy the two low level river crossings along this route that get you close to life along the river banks. I once saw a leopard in the shade of one of the bridges in the middle of the day. The route along the S36 passes further water holes. This productive route is a quieter alternative for guests moving on to Satara camp but still offers good game viewing. To the west of Skukuza camp the S3 again travels along the Sabie River. Being close to permanent water means that sightings are invariably good and this road is consistently productive for the big five. It is one of the quieter roads in terms of traffic. The S65, H1-1 and S114 to the south of Skukuza all offer good chances of the big five. The S114 also has a reputation for regular sightings of wild dog. Just off the H11, you should plan to spend some time at Lake Panic hide. This hide can be busy but is one of my favourite hides and is never missed from a trip to the Kruger. Here you are close to the waters edge, making this hide great for photography of hippo, crocodile and water birds.

The view from Lake Panic bird hide.

Morning drive

When wishing to return to Skukuza for breakfast, I find the loop that encompasses the H11, S1, S65 and H1-1 to be very rewarding. Stop at Lake Panic hide, just a short detour from the H11 along the S42. A popular hide, close views of hippos and water birds are guaranteed as you enjoy the sunrise. Even leopard are known to drink here. It is very easy to spend the morning here, but if you want to complete the loop you should move on after half an hour or so. Shortly after the H11 and S1 intersection is an active hyena den. Lion frequent this area too. They are also common along the S65, a picturesque road with good chances of seeing a variety of game. White rhino can often be spotted in the vicinity of De Laporte water hole on the H1-1. An alternative loop would be to take the H4-1, H12 and H1-2. Baboons are often seen around the bridge on the H12 and the entire loop offers fantastic opportunities for seeing just about anything. Birds are common along this loop too. The S83 loop can be a rewarding detour from the H1-2. Visibility can sometimes be poor, but lion, leopard and hyena sightings are reported frequently.

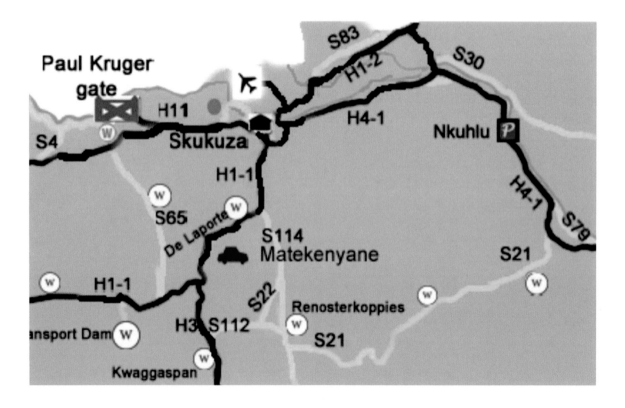

Further afield

The H4-1 to Lower Sabie is a good road at any time of the day. All of the large mammals, including the predators, are seen regularly along this route. You may get good sightings of some of the shy antelope, such as duiker, as they are habituated to the heavy traffic on this road. Nkhulu picnic site offers a welcome break with good views along this stretch of the river. Don't forget to spend some time at Sunset dam immediately before Lower Sabie rest camp. This spot can be busy with both traffic and animals and often you get very close views of animals coming to drink. The dam will also have the resident crocodiles and hippo for you to watch. The H1-2 can be taken from Skukuza towards Tshokwane picnic site. Lion can be seen regularly along this route. From the Kruger tablets onwards it can be a rewarding are for sightings. As you approach Tshokwane, zebra and wildebeest become more common. It is worth taking the short roads to each of the watering holes along this route. The S36, S34 and S33 to the north of the H1-2 offer further opportunities for game viewing. Rare antelope such as the Sable may be found along this first stretch of the S36. The S33 is a scenic route. Kudu, giraffe, warthog and buffalo are likely to be encountered here. By contrast the S34 can appear a little mundane, but the Munywini drainage line produces sweet grazing and has the potential for lion and leopard sightings. If following these routes north, return to Skukuza along the H1-2.

White Rhinoceros

Around Lower Sabie

Guests at Lower Sabie find game viewing easy, as all three of the main routes from the camp offer exceptional sightings. The H4-1 continues to be productive at this end of the route and along here, just one kilometre from camp, lies sunset dam. Here you can park your car very close to the waters edge and enjoy the many animals that come to visit. Look out for some very impressive crocodiles that will be sunning themselves on the banks of the dam. Heading south, the H4-2, S28, S82, S130 and S137 all cross through big five territory and will offer good sightings of a variety of game. The gravel roads in this area are quieter and I once viewed a cheetah on a kill, minutes from Lower Sabie along the S82, with only one other car for over an hour. Heading north, you first cross a low level bridge over the Sabie River. Given the opportunity, you could spend a long time here watching life along the river, including the hippo that are usually very close to the bridge. As you move onto the H10, sightings can be prolific. In the winter months, herbivore numbers increase in the region due to the good grazing available. In fact, this area is good for herbivore sightings of many species all year round. These high herbivore populations support large predator populations and all of the big cats are seen along this route. Towards the end of the H10 you climb to Nkumbe get out point. This is in many ways the most spectacular of the get out points in Kruger as the views here are truly stunning. The S29, S128 and S30 gravel roads all offer opportunities for good sightings. Along the S29, Mlondozi picnic site offers you a chance to stretch you legs whilst overlooking the impressive Mlondozi dam. I have had some good sightings here, including huge numbers of elephant, buffalo and zebra coming to drink.

This hippo was spotted from the low water bridge on the H10 outside Lower Sabie.

Morning drive

Talking the H4-1 to Skukuza for breakfast is very worthwhile. As described previously, sightings abound along this route. Equally productive are the roads to the south. This is big five country and all roads offer excellent chances of seeing these animals as well as cheetah and wild dog. All of these routes are described elsewhere. Another alternative is the H10 northwards. The open plains make for excellent viewing. Zebra and wildebeest are common. In the morning, hyenas are often found along the roadside where they have dens in roadside culverts. A wide variety of grazers exist here and this attracts plenty of lion. Cheetah are common along this road too. The H10 is another good road for rhino sightings. Look carefully around the intersection with the S129. Here reedbuck are usually found. They can be hard to spot, as they are most active in the early and later parts of the day. Take any of the gravel roads to return to Lower Sabie. The S128 and S129 have wide-open plains making game spotting easy. The S122 is a quiet road in terms of both sightings and traffic. Its interest lies in the fact that it traverses the Lebombo mountain bushveld and is one of a few in the park to do so. The S29 provides access to the Mlondozi picnic site that overlooks the Mlondozi dam. This is a rewarding place to spend some time, particularly from mid morning as the herds begin to gather to drink. The rest of the S29 is open vegetation, allowing good views of the many species that you may find here.

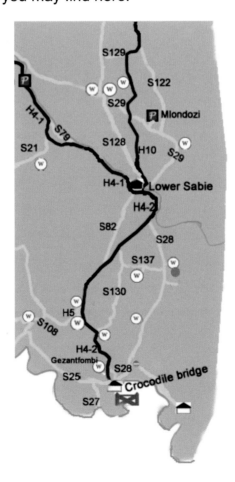

Further afield

Travelling the H10 up to Tshokwane picnic site is a must for all who stay at Lower Sabie. A rewarding road, it is likely that you will see elephant, rhino and buffalo. Giraffe and zebra are plentiful and lion sightings are often reported. Hyena are common too and cheetah will put in an appearance quite regularly. This is a picturesque road, but the jewel in the crown is towards the end. As you start to climb the Nkumbe hill, look out for klipspringer amongst the rocks. The Nkumbe viewpoint has spectacular views over the bush below and should not be missed. Lebombo euphorbias are seen growing on the slopes here. Spend some time, soak in the atmosphere and you will begin to spot a surprising number of animals below you. Orpen dam is a short detour from the H10 along the S32. This pleasing dam has shaded seating for you to watch animals coming to drink at the dam below and enjoy the surrounding bird life. Although this get out point has toilets, they are of the long drop variety. Rather travel onwards to Tshokwane and use the facilities there. Return to Lower Sabie by retracing your steps along the H10. You can take any of the gravel roads or for a longer journey you could take the H1-2 towards Skukuza, the H12 and H4-1 to return to camp.

Animals such as this rhino can be found close to the road in the Lower Sabie area.

Around Satara

Satara lies within open savannah grassland that supports a large diversity of animal and bird life. Even from the camp itself it is possible to see zebra, wildebeest and other animals coming to drink at the waterhole beyond the fence by the restaurant. The area is well populated with animals and the roads around camp are famous for the high frequency of lion sightings. Of these roads, it is the S100 that has the biggest reputation. Many guests have been rewarded with exceptional sightings of lion, leopard, cheetah and many other game species. However, this reputation means that the S100 is often a busy road, especially first thing in the morning. All the other routes from Satara also give you a good chance of seeing the big cats and can be better options to take early in the day if you wish to avoid a larger number of cars. An alternative to the S100, the H6 takes you to N'wanetsi picnic site. This productive road has in recent years been home to an active hyena den, offering close views of this often misunderstood species. The picnic site itself has a commanding view over a waterhole below that is often incredibly active with life. Only a short distance from here, along the S37, lies Sweni bird hide. This pleasant hide has good views over a waterhole and I can sit for hours watching the bird and animal life that visit. To the north, along the S41 lies Gudzani dam. You have a good chance of spotting many species here. Lion are reported in the area regularly. Heading south from Satara, the H1-3 can produce good sightings all the way to Tshokwane. Mazithi dam holds water all year round, is right next to the road and there is often much to view here. To the west, the S126 and S125 gravel roads carry less traffic but still offer good game viewing opportunities through big five country.

Also heading west towards Orpen, the H7 supports a wide variety of game and cheetah and lion are spotted regularly. Nsemani dam is found a short distance along this road from Satara. The road traverses what is essentially the dam wall and there is a short gravel track that leads to the back of the dam. There is always much to see here. The H1-4 heading north to Olifants is one of my favourites in the park and I never miss the opportunity to drive along it. You have a chance of seeing almost anything along this route and I have regularly seen the big cats here. The H1-4 has been my most consistently productive road for leopard. Another pleasant drive north, this time along the Timbavati River, is the S39. A long drive, you can join this route in three different places. I find this to be one of the most scenic drives in the park and game sightings have been good too. Along this route, I have enjoyed some peaceful moments watching game from Ratel Pan hide.

The main roads north and south of Satara have been productive places to spot leopards.

Morning drive

You are spoilt for choice when choosing your morning drive from Satara camp. All roads can produce special sightings. Many guests head south from camp in the morning and choose to drive the S100. This road is rated by many as one of the best in the park, consistently producing sightings of general game and all of the predators. This is because the road travels alongside the N'wanetsi river as it zigzags through the savannah. The riverine vegetation on one side and open plains of sweet grass on the other attract large numbers of game and make for easy game viewing. Birding is good throughout and you may be surprised at how long this 19km road can take to travel along. At the junction with the S41, head north for a few hundred metres and take in the views at the large Gudzani dam. From here you could head north on the S41 and take the S90 and H4-1 back to camp. The vegetation remains open and lion are often reported here. You should encounter plenty of zebra and wildebeest and grassland birds proliferate. However my preference would be to head south on the S41. The road passes by the Gudzani stream. Hippo are sometime present at the low water bridge and you may spot one of the kingfisher species. At the end of the S41, go to the N'wanetsi picnic site. Stretch your legs and walk up to the viewpoint, giving you elevated views over the Lebombo mountains and a stretch of the N'wanetsi river that is usually home to hippo and a variety of water birds. A short detour on the S37 will take you to Sweni hide. A variety of animals may come down to the waters edge to drink and there are usually hippo and crocodile to view. Return to Satara on the H6. Cheetah are regularly sighted on the open plains of this road. Look out for hyena around half way back to Satara. They have an active den here and clan members can often be found lounging next to the road. The section of the H1-3 that will take you back to camp runs parallel to the N'wanetsi river. Baboons are common here and leopard are seen in the riverine habitat.

Another option for a morning drive would be the S126. Drive south on the H1-3. The first section of this road passes riverine habitat and leopard can sometimes be seen from the bridges. The S126 can be quieter than other gravel roads in the area but is one of my favourites as it often offers up interesting sightings. The road follows the winding Sweni river. The eastern end is the most picturesque and you are likely to encounter giraffe, elephant, zebra and wildebeest on the open plains. Lion and leopard are seen frequently along the section up to Welverdiend waterhole. Visibility decreases a you approach the western section of the road and consequently game densities are lower and viewing is less prolific. Stop at the rustic Muzandzeni picnic site to stretch your legs before taking the S36 northwards. The open plains look like they should support a wide variety of grazers but I am yet to see much on this stretch of road. The H7 that will return you to Satara has a reputation as one of the best tar roads in the park. Lion, leopard and cheetah are common, as are the prey species. The Nsemani dam is large and close to the road. You can often see a variety of animals coming to drink from mid morning onwards.

A third option would be to take the H7 all the way to Orpen and back. You will pass through four ecozones, including open grassland and sections of mixed woodland before picking up the perennial Timbavati river. All the common game species should be present along this route. Predator sightings are common. As you get closer to Orpen you may have a chance of spotting wild dog. Elephant and white rhino are often spotted along this route too. Orpen is a very small camp that doubles as an entrance gate. On your return to Satara, you may want to take the S106 loop for a bit of variety. This road takes you past an old entrance gate to the park, the Rabelais hut. The road also passes Rabelais dam, where large herds often drink from mid morning. The dam is a little far from the road but game often cross the road on their way to the water source.

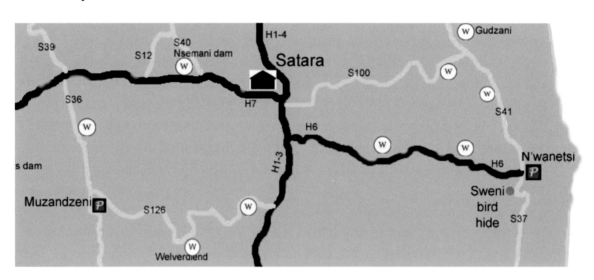

Further afield

Travelling the H1-4 in a morning is a must for me when staying at either Satara or Olifants. There are many water sources along this road and I have often spotted lion and leopard in the early mornings. Buffalo, elephant and warthog are regularly spotted too. The profusion of sightings along this road more than make up for the lacklustre scenery. As you get closer to Olifants camp you will cross the Olifants river. Here you can get out of your car in the demarcated area and admire the river below. Hippo, crocodile and a variety of water birds are often present here. Another road that is worthwhile taking is the S39. This is a very long road. The southern section, below the Timbavati picnic site, is less rewarding and game viewing opportunities are meagre. However the section north of the Timbavati picnic site is one of my favourites. As the road meanders along the route of the Timbavati river, there are many opportunities for good game viewing. Ratel pan hide overlooks a stretch of the river leading up to the Piet Grobler dam. Crocodile can usually be viewed at close quarters. As the road heads north, elephant and buffalo are usually plentiful. A wide variety of other species may also be seen. Zebra and giraffe are usually found in the vicinity of Goedgegun waterhole. The whole route offers a good chance of seeing lion and leopard.

Lion are common around Satara, making this a popular camp.

Around Olifants

Sitting astride the change in ecozones from open savannah to mopane woodland, Olifants camp offers diverse game viewing opportunities. From camp you have a remarkable view over the Olifants River below, and you can often spot game coming to drink. It is to the south of camp that I have had the consistently better sightings. From the camp, the H8 meanders down the hill towards the N'wamanzi lookout point over the river. I have seen lion several times along this road. Heading south along the H1-4 has produced consistently good sightings over the years. It is on this road that I have seen most of my leopard sightings. You can get out of your car at your own risk as the H1-4 crosses the Olifants River, allowing you to get up close and personal with the river. Just beyond here there is an active hyena den. I have also had good sightings of all of the other big five along this road too. The gravel roads to the south (S92, S91, S90, S89 and S39) also offer good chances of the big five and you will see many other species here too. To the north, sightings can be a bit slow, but browsers such as Kudu are common and you should see hippo and elephant along the riverine routes.

Leopard on the Olifants to Satara road.

Morning drive

If you wish to return to Olifants for breakfast then I would recommend that you take the S92 around three kilometres from camp. This road follows the Olifants river. It can be very corrugated and sightings can often be slow, however you are likely to see elephant along this route. The real gem of taking this route is the low water bridge across the Olifants river at Balule. Here you can get very close to a variety of water birds and often hippo too. Take the S90 south and then the S89. At the intersection of these roads there are often hyena that have an active den a short way along the S90. The S89 is a short road that consistently produces sightings of giraffe, zebra and waterbuck. Lion and leopard have been spotted along this road too. The H1-4 and H8 will take you back to Olifants camp.

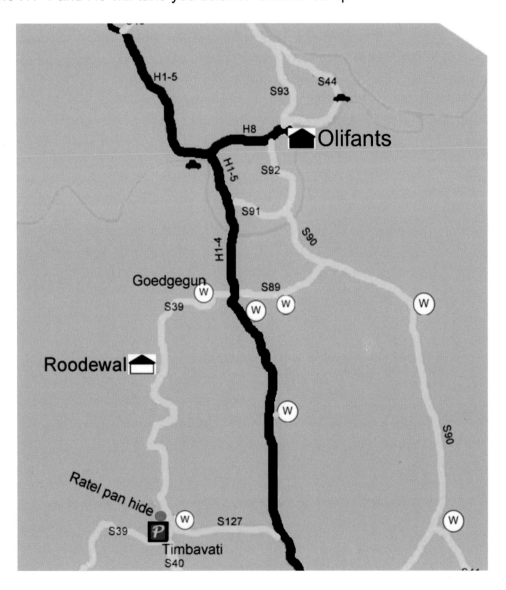

Further afield

Game densities are lower as you head north of north of Olifants. The S44 makes its way to a spectacular lookout over the Olifants river. There is plenty of birdlife to occupy you, but animal sightings can be few and far between away from the river. Game viewing along the S93 is better when the road links up with the Letaba river. You may spot giraffe and elephant are common. Closer to Letaba, the S46 and S94 gravel routes are often quiet. Elephant and buffalo may be encountered but other game species are scarce. The H1-5 that you will return to camp on is another slow road. Game densities within the mopane veld are low. The best section of this road is the section that runs alongside the Olifants river. Huge herds of buffalo come to drink, elephant and hippo are plentiful and you have a good chance of spotting lion and hyena.

A better option from Olifants is to head south. Both the H1-4 and S39 are excellent routes and are described in the Satara section. The S90 is also worthwhile. Open plains are home to zebra, wildebeest and buffalo and grassland birds are plentiful. Steenbok are very obvious here too. There is a fair chance of spotting lion along this road.

Around Letaba

Overlooking a wide expanse of the 'river of sand', Letaba marks the start of the area where you may begin to encounter the 'big tuskers' of Kruger – male elephants that are carrying an impressive set of ivory. Game is not as prolific as in the south, but you can expect to see a good variety of animals, including large herds of buffalo and impressive elephants, even if it proves more difficult to see all of the big five. The route along the H1-6 immediately north of camp follows the path of the Letaba River. Here you can expect to see a wide variety of animals living alongside the river and in the early morning you have the best chance of spotting lion and leopard. You can get out of your car at your own risk between the demarcated points on the Letaba river bridge. I find the Letaba bridge to offer very scenic views of the river below with a good chance of seeing elephant. The S48 Tsendze loop is regarded by many as the most productive route in the area, especially in the dry season. At this time, water often remains in the riverbed, attracting a wide variety of animals that depend upon it and so do not move very far. The drive along the S47 to Mingerhout dam is usually fruitful. However, this dam is quite far from the road and it is animals moving to and from this dam that you will be able to spot. Moving further afield, both the H9 and H14 can offer rewarding sightings, including leopard and wild dog, although opportunities for game viewing can be patchy along both routes.

Morning drive

At the junction outside of camp, turn right and follow the H1-6 as it accompanies the Letaba river. This is one of the best stretches of road in the area. A variety of game, including elephant and giraffe, are usually visible. In the riverbed, look out for hippos and waterbuck. You have a good chance of spotting lion and leopard here early in the morning. Before the bridge, take the S47 road to the Mingerhout dam. Game viewing can be variable. You may encounter large herds of buffalo and elephant. Continue on the S47 until you meet up with the S131 that you will use to return to camp. Just before the crossroads outside Letaba, look out for hyena that often den in the area.

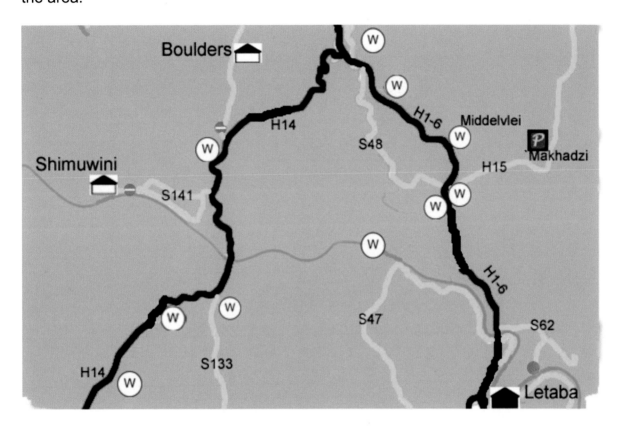

Further afield

The H9 links Letaba with Phalaborwa gate. Game viewing can be sporadic but there is always hippo in the dams along the route. Many visitors have had luck with lion, leopard and wild dog along this route, but I have always found it quiet in terms of game sightings. Masorini archaeological site is worth visiting. You may take a guided tour to find out how Stone Age man utilised this area. Klipspringer can usually be found on the rocky outcrop. As you get closer to Phalaborwa, take the S51 detour to Sable dam and overnight hide. Water birds are common and you will usually be able to spot impala, buffalo and elephant in the vicinity of the dam. The H14 follows a scenic route to the north. Game densities remain low on this road but the low water bridge crossing the Letaba river is worthwhile. Here you can spend some time watching the hippo and water birds. Buffalo and elephant are likely to be encountered along the length of this route.

Heading north towards Mopani on the H1-6 can be rewarding. All of the waterholes along the way attract game. You should see zebra and have a fair chance of spotting Tsessebe, one of the rare antelopes in the park. Of the waterholes, Middelvlei is the most rewarding. From early mornings onwards a steady stream of game comes to the water hole. Large elephant bulls are also often attracted here. The S48 is a scenic drive along the perennial Tsendze river. Elephant and buffalo herds are common and you may see a variety of animal and bird life.

Large tuskers roam the area north of Letaba.

Around Mopani

As is typical of the north, game densities around Mopani camp are low. However there are still opportunities for some exceptional game viewing and I never miss out on visiting this area when I am planning a trip. The camp itself overlooks Pioneer dam and you can watch life take its course here from your hut or the restaurant area. The S142 travels behind this dam, passing two bird hides in Pioneer hide and Shipandani hide. Both allow you the opportunity to sit quietly and watch game coming to drink. Of these, I prefer Shipandani. The resident hippo here and the closeness of the hide to the water make for good animal and bird spotting. A short distance to the south from Mopani camp, Mooiplaas picnic site is often very quiet. However, it gives you a rustic bush experience and the bird and animal life along the riverine habitat is good. To the east, the S143 and S50 are not to be missed. Large bull elephants roam this area and it is along these roads that you have the best opportunity to see some of the rare antelope such as Roan, Tsessebe and Eland.

Look out for rare antelope such as this Tsessebe in the Mopani area.

Morning drive

Head north on the H1-6 towards Shingwedzi. Zebra, buffalo and elephant are common along this stretch of road. The tropic of Capricorn is well marked on this route and is an informative place to get out of your vehicle at your own risk. Take the S144 to link up with the S143. The S144 is usually quiet, but sightings pick up along the S143 where you may spot ostrich, zebra, wildebeest and possibly even the elusive eland and roan antelope. The S143 has open plains for much of its duration. Picking up the S50, which follows the Nshawu drainage line, sightings continue to be good. Elephant bulls are often found in this this marshy area. Take the road past Mooiplaas waterhole to return to camp. Many animals favour this waterhole and there are often zebra and wildebeest milling around.

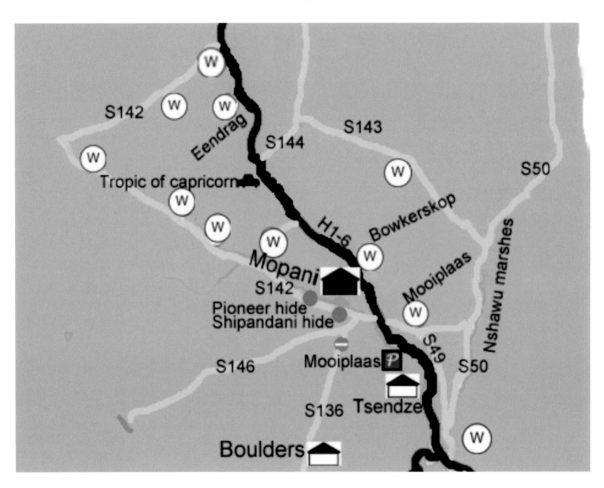

Further afield

When staying at Mopani you must try to visit Shingwedzi camp. The H1-6 that will take you there goes through mopane veld. Game densities are low, but elephant and buffalo are regularly seen. Lion also put in an occasional appearance. It is at the waterholes along this route that many animals congregate at from mid morning onwards. Bowkerskop, Gyrsbok and Eendrag attract fair numbers of game that often stay in the area after drinking. Game viewing picks up as the road runs parallel to the Shingwedzi river. Giraffe, baboon, vervet monkey and buffalo may all be present. The short stretch of road leading to Shingwedzi is prolific for animal and bird sightings and you are likely to see many elephant in the riverbed below.

Closer to Mopani, do not miss out on visiting the Shipandani overnight hide on the S142. On the way to this hide you will cross a low water bridge, allowing you very close views of water birds and crocodile. The hide itself sits in an enviable position close to the waters edge. The rest of the S142 can be slow going in terms of animal sightings.

Buffalo in the Mopane veld surrounding Mopani camp

Around Shingwedzi

Shingwedzi enjoys the reputation as being the best game viewing area in the north of the park. A wide variety of game is attracted to the river, including large elephant bulls. Lion are also frequently seen in the area and leopards are often reported along the S50. This road closely follows the Shingwedzi River. You should drive slowly as this is a scenic but narrow road and animals, including elephant, can appear out of nowhere. In fact, many roads around Shingwedzi are scenic river routes. To the south, the S52 takes you along the river to the red rocks lookout point. I have never seen anything noteworthy here but I find the place to be extremely beautiful. Leopard and lion are seen here from time to time. To the north, the S56 Mphongolo road along the usually dry river of the same name is a rewarding drive. Once again scenic, game is quite abundant and you have a good chance of seeing buffalo and elephant. Even if game is scarce, bird life along this route is prolific.

Morning drive

There are many good riverine routes to take in the morning from Shingwedzi. Many people drive the S50 from the back gate of the camp. This road follows the Shingwedzi river. You may want to take a sort detour to the low level crossing just outside of camp as this often provides close up viewing of water birds and crocodile. Look out for nyala and bushbuck along the banks of the river as you traverse the S50. Vegetation can be dense; elephant are common and can appear quickly on the road in front of you. The Kanniedood dam and bird hide offer good views over the river and a chance of seeing elephant, buffalo and other animals and birds that live close to water. Many visitors turn around and retrace their steps at the dam or a little further on at the Dipeni outpost as the roads leaves the river. From here the sightings on the S50 going south are less rewarding.

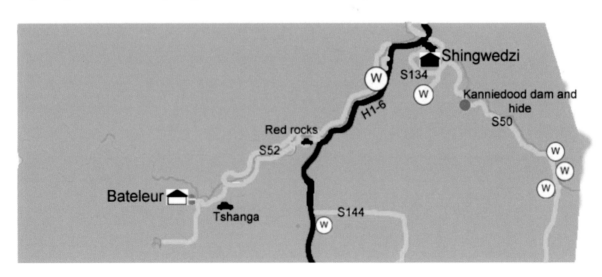

Further afield

The S52 takes in two lovely look out points in Tshanga and red rocks. It is a long route that follows the course of the Shingwedzi river. Pools of water are often visible in the riverbed below and impala and warthog are common. Tshanga offers an endless view over the mopane veld and red rocks is a part of the river with unusual red rocks that lend the look out point its name. Buffalo and elephant will most likely be encountered along the route.

Further north the H1-7 and S56 make a pleasing loop to drive. The H1-7 drives through mostly mopane veld. The corresponding low game densities can make game scarce, but as with everywhere in the north you have a good chance of seeing buffalo and elephant. You may even see the rare eland. Close to camp you may see impala and giraffe. Lion are reported here and hyena is frequently spotted in the early mornings and evenings. The S55 is a worthwhile short detour at the start of the H1-7. Predator sightings are more frequent on this road as many animals cross to get access to the river. On the H1-7, stop at Babalala picnic site to stretch legs and take on refreshments under the inviting sycamore fig tree. From here take the S56. This Mphongolo route follows the course of the river and there are many spectacular tree specimens to admire. Game viewing can be variable, but nyala and bushbuck are usually plentiful. I would also expect to see kudu, buffalo and elephant on this route.

Zebra on the H1-6

70

Around Punda Maria

A very peaceful camp a long way from the hustle and bustle of the south of the park, Punda Maria offers easy access to the most northern areas of the park. The circular S99 can produce some good sightings, including nyala, buffalo, elephant and leopard, but can be rather inconsistent. From Punda Maria, make the journey to the Pafuri area: it is a must for any visitor to northern Kruger. It is incredibly scenic and bird life is prolific, including species such as crested guinea fowl and trumpeter hornbills that are not found in other parts of the park. Pafuri picnic spot is not to be missed. Further scenic loops along the Luvuvhu river take you to Crook's corner on the Limpopo river, a get out point that is rich in history for lawbreakers trying to escape the authorities at the meeting point of South Africa, Mozambique and Zimbabwe. Here large crocodiles bask in the sun.

Morning drive

A good circular route back to camp is the S99 that is equally good in any direction. A picturesque loop, you may see animals, birds and plant species that are not found elsewhere in the park. Look out for the rare Sharpe's grysbok. You should also encounter elephant, buffalo, impala and kudu. However, predator sightings on this route are uncommon.

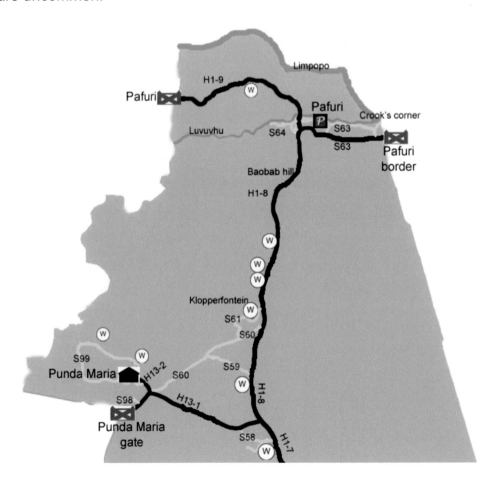

Further afield

Whilst staying at Punda Maria you must visit the Pafuri region along the Luvuvhu river. Take the S60 from camp. You may see zebra along this road, but impala and buffalo are common. It is worth taking the S61 as a detour to the Klopperfontein dam. Elephant commonly drink here and the waterhole forms a focal point for game in the immediate vicinity. The H1-8 will take you north towards Pafuri. Animals are scarce along this stretch of road. As you pass the often-photographed baobab hill you start to descend into the Luvuvhu flood plains. Game densities increase near the river and you will be pleasantly surprised by the variety of game that you spot. Don't forget to park on the bridge overlooking the river to see what animals have come for a drink below. Take the S63 towards Crook's corner. This has both tarred and sand branches but it is the sand section that is more rewarding. The Pafuri picnic site is a tranquil place where birdlife abounds. Nyala are common on the winding road with a tropical feel, but predators are scarce. Crook's corner gives you the opportunity to view some huge crocodiles. Retrace your steps to return to Punda Maria.

Staying at bushveld camps

If you are fortunate to stay in one of the quieter bushveld camps, you will utilise many of the routes associated with the closest main rest camps. However, some of these bushveld camps have roads that are exclusive for guests staying at the camp.

At Biyamiti in the south of Kruger, guests have exclusive use of the S139. The road follows the meandering path of the Biyamiti river. Sightings can be exceptional. If you are staying at Biyamiti it is advisable to explore this road thoroughly. Leopards are seen regularly as are all of the big five. It is a very rewarding road at all times of the year.

Talamati is situated on the plains between Orpen and Satara camps. The S145 attracts large herds of zebra that drink at Fairfield waterhole. Other game is plentiful and this attracts predators, most notably lion, but cheetah are fairly regularly seen too.

Shimuwini camp, northwest of Letaba, enjoys the private S141. The section that follows the river is more productive and you can be sure that buffalo and elephant will be in the area.

Bateleur and Sirheni bushveld camps are not far from Shingwedzi. If staying here you should consider the routes outlined in the Shingwedzi section.

Lion in the long grass.

4.6: Other ways to spend your time.

Although much of your time will be spent out on the roads of Kruger, there are still many other ways of spending your time. Whilst in camp you may want to take advantage of the many facilities. This includes the swimming pools that are found in all main rest camps, or browsing the shops for souvenirs. As you walk around the camps you are able to enjoy the abundant bird life and in some camps, such as Letaba, there are resident mammals such as bushbuck. Don't miss the many historical sites in Skukuza camp or the enjoyable and informative elephant hall at Letaba camp. Camps set alongside rivers offer a chance to sit and relax whilst enjoying the comings and goings along the river. Outside of the rest camps you may want to spend some time at one of the picnic sites. These offer a variety of refreshments and food and many are situated in ideal locations for watching wildlife. You can also spend some time in one of the many hides overlooking a game viewing spot such as a waterhole. At night, the main camps show wildlife movies in an open-air amphitheatre. If you want to get out of the camps but don't want to drive yourself, there are a few options open to you.

Guided drives:

Sunset drives: these drives set out shortly before the sun sets and return in the dark, allowing you see animals at dusk and at the start of the night. These drives are great for nocturnal activity and return to camp before the restaurants shut, giving you time to eat your meal before you retire to bed. Check with your camp or the nearest gate for availability.

Night drives: leaving after the sunset drives return, you will get to see nocturnal animals go about their business. This is ideal for spotting animals such as porcupine or civet that can be hard to spot during the day. Check with your camp or the nearest gate for availability. Drives last around three hours.

Morning drives: leave before the sun rises to be first out on the roads and possibly encounter nocturnal animals as they finish their activity in the first light of the day. Drives last for three to four hours.

Guided walks

Guided walks are available from most camps, where groups of up to eight people explore the bush on foot for a few hours, guided by armed, experienced rangers, getting up close and personal with the wildlife. Although you might see some of the larger animals, these walks give you an opportunity to enjoy the small creatures that you might miss from your vehicle. Both morning walks in the hours after dawn and afternoon walks leading up to dusk are available. Olifants camp also offers a daytime river walk.

Wilderness trails

These overnight trails allow adventurous travellers the opportunity for a true bush experience. There are seven trail locations throughout the park, each catering for a maximum of eight guests, and each trail lasts for three nights. The two days in between are spent exploring the surrounding area on foot. The trail locations are:

Bushman: situated in the valleys and hills of the Berg-en-dal region.

Metsi-metsi: walking in the game rich area to the east of Tshokwane picnic site. Check in is at Skukuza.

Napi: this trail lies in the picturesque landscape between Pretoriuskop and Skukuza.

Nyalaland: an area of rich botanic diversity, including some giant baobab trees, this trail is in the far north of the park.

Olifants: departing from Letaba camp, this trail is set on the banks of the Olifants River, close to its confluence with the Letaba River.

Sweni: in big cat country, this trail covers the open plains to the southeast of Satara camp.

Wolhuter: named after one of the first rangers, this trail lies in the south west of the park.

Back-pack trails

The Olifants river, Mphongolo and Lonely Bull backpack trails offer primitive camping in which guests are expected to provide their own tents and food for the four day, three night excursions.

4x4 adventure trails

Only six vehicles per day may traverse these trails. They give you an opportunity to get off the regular tourist roads. Although your 4x4 skills will not be tested, these trails are limited to 4x4 vehicles to reduce the impact on the environment. The Mananga trail, beginning a short distance from Satara, is currently the only operational trail. The trail is weather dependent and can only be booked on the day that you travel on it.

Eco-trails

The Malopeni overnight eco-trail is a guided one-night adventure trail that travels along park management roads in the area to the northeast of Phalaborwa Gate up to the Letaba River. The Lebombo eco-trail is an outdoor adventure that follows the eastern boundary of the Kruger National Park along the Lebombo hills and lasts for four nights.

Bush braais and breakfasts

A short game drive will take you into the bush where your meal will be served with your ranger as your host. Another short game drive follows on your return to camp. For bush braais this will be in the dark and you will be able to view nocturnal animals.

Mountain bike trails

Departing from Olifants camp only, these trails use mountain bikes to explore the surrounding flora and fauna. Both morning and afternoon trails are available. A certain level of fitness is advised as these trails cover at least twenty kilometres over sometimes difficult terrain.

Golf

A short drive from Skukuza camp you will find Skukuza golf course, a nine hole, eighteen tee course in the African bush. As the course is not fenced you should expect to see some of the local wildlife as you play. Clubs, buggies and caddies are available for hire.

Food

Each accommodation unit in the park comes with its own braai stand. Here you can barbecue your own dinner. Alternatively, you can use the kitchen facilities in your bungalow or the communal kitchen facilities. All shops are well stocked with groceries to make a fulfilling meal. If you don't want to cater for yourself there are take away and eat in restaurants offering wholesome meals at all main camps.

Using the braai at Satara camp.

Section five: photography.

Going on safari is an exciting trip and for many, a once in a lifetime opportunity. You will want to take pictures and videos of all that you see. With a bit of thought and practice, you can turn standard holiday snaps into good wildlife photographs. Be sure to look at the big five photographic tips first. This section will give you further ideas to think about.

Top photography tips:

Know your camera before you go. As many animal sightings are fleeting, you don't want to miss a photo or have your photos ruined by not knowing your camera. Make sure you have had plenty of practice before you go.

Spend your money on lenses, not the camera. An average lens will always produce average photographs, regardless of how good the camera body is. Buy the best quality lens with the longest focal length that you can afford.

Use the light. In the early mornings and late evenings the soft light adds golden warmth to your pictures, whereas midday light is harsh and produces lots of shadows. Be creative at these times and use fill in flash where possible to reduce shadows. Of course, dull overcast days can still be good for photography as the light is soft and diffuse.

Use a wide aperture. This will give you a faster shutter speed to freeze the action as well as blurring the background, making the animal or bird stand out against the thick bush behind it.

Support your camera properly. This can be tricky whilst in the car as the small vibrations from a running engine can have a big impact on your photos. Turn the engine off and use a window support such as a beanbag to ensure that you get sharp pictures every time.

The early bird

In terms of wildlife photography, it is most definitely the early bird that catches the worm. Plan to be out of the camp gate as early as possible. In the first hour or so after the sun rises, the light will have a golden glow that will add warmth and texture to your photographs. It is also at this time that predators are most active and you have your best chances of taking an interesting photograph of them. The same can be said for the last hour of light in the day. At this time, golden warmth returns to the light and once again predators start to become active.

Direction

If photography is your main reason for visiting Kruger, it is worth planning your trips from camp by considering the position of the sun. If travelling east in the morning, the sun will be directly in front of you and behind any animals that you encounter on the road. By travelling west, the light falls onto the animals from behind you. Both situations can produce interesting photographs. Arguably, back and side lit photographs are the most interesting but it is a harder skill to master when the sun is directly behind an animal.

Depth of field

If there is one skill to master before your safari it is knowing how to control the depth of field (the amount of your photograph that is in focus) through changing the aperture. In many areas of Kruger the bush can be quite dense and you want to make the animal that you are photographing stand out. You can do this by using the aperture priority mode on your camera and changing the aperture size. The aperture is the size of the opening of the iris diaphragm in your camera. It is measured in f-stops, for example f2.8, f4, f5.6. A wide-open aperture of f2.8 would give a very shallow depth of field with only your focus point in focus whereas an aperture of f22 would give a larger depth of field with much of your photograph in focus. You can use a small f-stop number to make your subject stand out from the surrounding bush.

Producing really sharp images

It is always disappointing to take your pictures only to find out at a later time that they are not as sharp as you had wished for. A few simple tips can lead to sharper photographs. With wildlife photography, it is the eyes that are most important and these should be the focus point for tightly framed shots of animals. By using a small f-stop for your aperture you will also have a fast shutter speed. This will help to freeze the action. You can also take control of this in your camera if you want to create more artistic shots such as a blurred pan. Try to support your camera when taking photographs. In your car, this is best done with a beanbag that rests over the door when the window is open. Using a shutter release cable can also help to remove any unwanted movement. Make sure that your engine is switched off when it is safe to do so as small engine moments can cause blurry photographs. If you do have to hand hold your camera, make sure that the shutter speed is the same or greater than the lens focal length. For a 300mm lens this would mean a speed of 1/300th of a second or more.

Exposures

Modern day cameras are excellent at judging exposures, but still need a little help with very dark or very light subjects. When photographing an animal such as buffalo, underexpose your picture slightly so that the animals appear black and not grey. Similarly, a bird that is completely white may look grey unless you overexpose slightly.

Composition: making not taking

Photographs where your subject is in the centre of frame can look uninteresting. Try to experiment with where your subject lies in the picture. One way to start doing this is to apply the 'rule of thirds', where you place your subject along lines that split the picture into thirds both horizontally and vertically. When you get more confident you can abandon this rule and look to experiment. Once you have taken a few photographs, look for different angles and try different ideas. After taking a few tightly framed shots, try some wider angles that show your subject within its environment.